AFRICAN SOCIETY TODAY
The African worker

FEB 1 1 2004

Published by the Press Syndicate of the University of Cambridge
The Pitt Building, Trumpington Street, Cambridge CB2 1RP
32 East 57th Street, New York, NY 10022, USA
10 Stamford Road, Oakleigh, Melbourne 3166, Australia

First published 1988

Printed in Great Britain at the University Press, Cambridge

British Library cataloguing in publication data
Freund, Bill
The African worker. – (African society today)
1. Africa south of the Sahara. Employment. Labour, to 1987
I. Title II. Series
331′.0967

Library of Congress cataloguing in publication data
Freund, Bill.
The African worker.
(African society today)
Bibliography.
Includes index.
1. Labor and laboring classes – Africa. I. Title. II. Series.
HD8776.5.F74 1988 305.5′62′096 87-38102

ISBN 0 521 30758 9 hard covers
ISBN 0 521 31491 7 paperback